Owl Life

by Kara Race-Moore

PEARSON Scott Foresman

DK

What You Already Know

Living things interact to get energy. All living things need energy to live and grow. Producers are living things that can use the Sun to make their own energy. Consumers eat producers or other consumers in order to get energy.

Herbivores are consumers that only eat plants. Carnivores are consumers that only eat animals. Consumers that get eaten by predators become the prey of those predators. Some carnivores can also be prey. Omnivores eat both plants and animals.

Food chains are made up of producers and consumers interacting and passing on energy. When a consumer eats a producer, it gets that producer's energy. Later on, that consumer may become prey to another consumer. Two consumers are in competition when they are both trying to get the same resources.

The food chain continues when a living thing dies and decays. Decomposers, such as mushrooms, break down dead plants and animals, along with waste. Decomposers help prevent the spread of germs and disease by removing waste.

Owls are birds. They have their own special ways to find food, make shelter for themselves, stay safe from other animals, and more. Keep reading to find out everything there is to know about owls!

Owls are carnivores.

Owl Life

Owls are unique birds with many special adaptations. All owls have similar features in common. They have large, forward facing eyes, a rounded head, short tail, and stiff, upright posture. Owls are able to fly quietly with their large wings.

Owls have also adapted in ways that help them survive in different habitats. Owls can be found in many different places in the world, including deserts and the polar tundra.

There are over two hundred species of owls. They range in size from the tiny elf owl, which is about the same size as a sparrow, to the eagle owl, which can have a wingspan of six feet. Even with so many owls, it is rare for people to see them. This is because most owls are active only at night.

Owls have undergone many adaptations that have made them excellent predators. The two most important adaptations are probably their great hearing and eyesight. Even though owls can see very well at night, they usually rely on their hearing to find their prey.

Owls can be found all over the world. Most sleep during the day, which makes it difficult for people to spot them.

Owl Habitats

Owls live all over the world in many different habitats. Tawny owls, like most kinds of owls, live in forests. They make their nests in tree hollows and come out at night to hunt. During the day tawny owls sleep on tree branches. This is in contrast to many other birds that are active during the day. Arctic owls, also called snowy owls, live on the Arctic tundra. They make nests on the ground. To withstand the cold, snowy owls have a dense covering of feathers. They even have feathers on their toes!

Snowy owls have white feathers with black specks.

The tawny owl swoops down from tall trees to hunt its prey.

Burrowing owls live in the grasslands and prairies where there is open ground. They make their nests in the abandoned burrows of animals such as woodchucks, skunks, and prairie dogs. Unlike most types of owls, burrowing owls will often come outside during the day. They hunt and eat insects as well as prairie rodents.

Burrowing owls use their long legs to walk on the prairies.

Night Hunter

Most owls are nocturnal. Some owls spend most of their nights out hunting, away from their nests. Other owls sing for most of the night, only hunting at dusk and dawn. As an owl approaches its prey, it spreads its wings as wide as they will stretch. The owl thrusts its large claws forward to grab the animal. Once an owl has successfully caught its prey, it will immediately start to eat it, unless the owl is catching food for its young.

Owls hunt alone. Different owls have different hunting methods depending on their prey and their habitat. Owls that live in the woods will often stay perched on a branch for a long time, listening for the sound of their prey. Owls that hunt on grassland, however, will fly around until they find their prey. Some owls have unique hunting methods. The bay owl will sometimes wait inside a bat cave. When a bat tries to fly out, it will be captured!

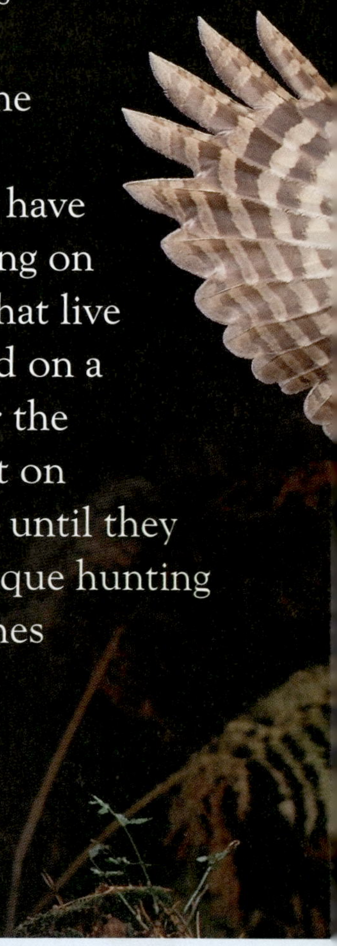

Owls are able to use their feathers as camouflage to keep other animals from seeing them. When owls hear a mouse or vole or some other prey moving, they attack suddenly and silently. Owls have large mouths, but they don't have any teeth. They tear up their prey with curved bills that act like pliers. They eat all of it.

Owls are so stealthy that they may have a hard time seeing each other! To let other owls know they are there, they may sing, clap they wings together, or snap their bills.

This owl spreads out its wings in preparation for a landing.

Silent Flight

A barn owl's wings allow it to glide slowly while it searches for prey.

Owls fly silently through the air. Because their wings are rounded, they are not able to fly as fast as some birds. Owls make up for this with their ability to fly very quietly. They are able to fly in near silence because their wings have specially adapted feathers. These feathers help to quiet any sound the owls might make while they are moving through the air.

The owl's feathers are very soft and velvety. Many kinds of owls have fringed edges on their wingtip feathers. The soft texture and tattered edges helps the feathers to move through the air without creating a large wake.

Large air wakes are what cause sound. Owl feathers break large air wakes up into smaller wakes. The smaller wakes make much less sound. This helps the owl to create as little noise as possible while in flight. That way the prey won't hear the owl coming.

The owl's wingtips have special features that help the owl fly as silently as possible.

Easy Prey

What do you think owls like to eat? Many people think of mice when they think of an owl's favorite food. Owls do eat mice, but they also eat many other kinds of animals.

An owl's diet can include different types of rodents, smaller birds, fish, frogs, and insects such as grasshoppers and beetles. Larger owls such as the snowy owl and eagle owl will hunt for larger birds. They will even search out birds such as heron and small mammals such as foxes for prey. Smaller owls often catch moths in mid-air.

Owls eat many smaller animals, such as frogs and mice.

frog

mouse

The bones and fur from this owl's prey will later be turned into pellets like those on the right.

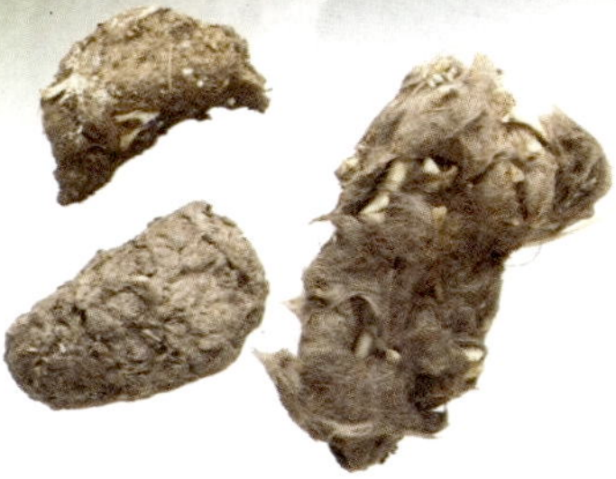

owl pellets

Owls digest the parts of their prey that provide them with energy. The rest of the animal, which the owl has no use for, gets coughed up as pellets. Pellets contain everything the owl could not digest, including the bones and fur.

Owl Adaptations

Owls have developed many adaptations, which help them survive. Excellent eyesight and hearing, very sharp bills and claws, and feathers are all important adaptations.

Camouflage

Most owls sleep during the day. By hiding in trees and not making any movements, owls stay safe from daytime predators. Owls' feathers also have special markings that help keep them from being seen by the animals that hunt them. The markings, along with the feathers' color patterns, help owls blend into their habitat. Often, the colors of the feathers match the colors of the trees that the owls sleep in. This camouflage makes the owls even harder for predators to see.

This owl's feathers help camouflage it while it sleeps in the tree.

Claws and Beaks

The owl's claws are perfect for holding things.

Owls have extremely powerful claws and bills that enable them to catch prey quickly.

Owls' claws, or talons, are flexible and very sharp. Their claws are also very strong, so strong that they rarely break when the owl uses them to grab prey. Owls can flex their claws out and then curl them in to better help them catch and hold onto prey.

The owl's short hooked bill helps the owl tear at its prey. It also makes it easier for the owl to see where it's going when it has food in its mouth.

The owl's sharp bill is well adapted for hunting.

Eyesight

Owls' eyes are on the front of their faces. Many other animals have their eyes on the sides of their faces. Part of the reason that owls have excellent vision and are great hunters is because of the location and the size of their eyes.

Because owls are not able to move their eyes in their sockets, they are forced to turn their heads in order to follow a moving object. They can almost turn their heads in a full circle!

Much of the space in an owl's skull is taken up by its eye sockets.

Owls' eyes face front, allowing them to see how far away their prey is.

Hearing

Owls can hear very well. Some of them can hunt by sound alone. Owl faces are shaped elliptically, like a satellite dish. This shape helps their ears take in as much sound as possible. Owls also have special feathers on their faces that help make sounds louder. Not only that, but the owl's left and right ear differ in shape and position. Because of this, the ears are able to pick up different noises from different places, helping owls locate their prey.

The tufts on owls' heads look like ears, but they are just feathers.

Owlets

Owls make their nests in dark burrows and tree hollows. When they finish making their nests, they lay their eggs. Owls' eggs are usually white. The white color makes it easier for the parents to see the eggs. The mother owl incubates the eggs for about a month.

tawny owl egg

Parents guard the owlets until they are big enough to take care of themselves.

When owlets hatch, they are totally dependent on their parents for food. At first, the father owl is responsible for bringing food to the nest. The mother owl takes the food that the father owl has brought and feeds the owlets small pieces. Once the owlets are able to swallow food whole, the mother owl will go hunting for them also.

Owlets are born with soft, warm feathers called down. They will often explore the nest area by walking and climbing around. Owlets fly off from their parents and the nest soon after they grow their first adult feathers. They usually grow their adult feathers when they are a few months old.

young Iranian eagle owls

Different Owls

There are many different kinds of owls. They live all over the world. Each owl has its own special adaptations and behaviors. These traits help owls to survive in the many different habitats where they live.

Eagle owls are one of the largest types of owls. They are very good night hunters.

Snowy owls live in some of the coldest climates on Earth.

The Bengal eagle owl gets its name from Bengal, an area in India.

Spectacled owls like to live near water in tropical rain forests.

Snowy owls have thick feathers all over their bodies. These feathers help keep them warm on the cold tundra. Spectacled owls are found in both humid rain forests and cooler woodlands. They eat insects, reptiles, birds, crabs, and rodents.

The barn owl is found almost worldwide. It is named for its habit of making its nest in barns. Farmers encourage barn owls to roost near their farms. Barn owls catch and eat rodents that ruin crops. They are among the most common owls in the world.

Amazing Owls

Owls are amazing birds. They have special adaptations that allow them to hunt at night, catch their prey in complete darkness, and camouflage themselves while they sleep during the day. They can fly silently through the air, and they have excellent hearing and eyesight. They can pinpoint their prey simply by listening and can see long distances at night or in the day.

Buffy fish owl

Owls are very flexible. Their necks allow them to turn their heads up to 270 degrees. Owls' claws are specially adapted so they can extend and curl to snatch up their prey.

Owls are found all over the world and are adapted to live in many different conditions. They eat many different types of small animals whole. Owls are extraordinary predators as well as beautiful nocturnal birds.

barn owl

Glossary

down soft, warm, feathers grown by young birds before they are able to fly

elliptical having a shape like an oval with both ends alike

incubate to keep warm

pellet a compact ball of all the parts of an animal that an owl could not digest

posture a position of the body or way of holding the body

sockets the hollow areas of the skull where the eyeballs are located

talons the claws of predatory birds

wake the way air is moved or disturbed when something passes through it